Please return/renew this item by the
last date shown to avoid a charge.
Books may also be renewed by phone
and Internet. May not be renewed if
required by another reader.

www.libraries.barnet.gov.uk

LONDON BOROUGH

History in Living Memory

Getting Around
Through the Years

How transport
has changed in
living memory

Clare Lewis

raintree

a Capstone company — publishers for children

Raintree is an imprint of Capstone Global Library Limited, a company incorporated in England and Wales having its registered office at 7 Pilgrim Street, London, EC4V 6LB – Registered company number: 6695582

www.raintree.co.uk
myorders@raintree.co.uk

Edited by Clare Lewis and Holly Beaumont
Designed by Philippa Jenkins
Picture research by Tracy Cummins
Production by Victoria Fitzgerald
Originated by Capstone Global Library Ltd
Printed and bound in China by Leo Paper Group

ISBN 978 1 406 29013 4
18 17 16 15 14
10 9 8 7 6 5 4 3 2 1

British Library Cataloguing in Publication Data
A full catalogue record for this book is available from the British Library.

Acknowledgements
We would like to thank the following for permission to reproduce photographs: Capstone Press: Philippa Jenkins, 1 Right, 1 Top Left; Corel: Reuben T. Parsons, 4; Getty Images: AFP PHOTO/JIJI PRESS, 12, Alexis DUCLOS/Gamma-Rapho, 16, Car Culture ® Collection, 19, Dennis Oulds/Central Press, 14, Fox Photos, 15, Lambert, 10, The AGE/Fairfax Media, 8, The Denver Post, 7; Glow Images: Superstock, 11; Shutterstock: Everett Collection, 5, Flas100, Design Element, Hung Chung Chih, 17, Back Cover, i4lcocl2, 23 Bottom, kaczor58, 23 Middle, Maksim Toome, 22 Top Right, Monkey Business Images, 20, Olegusk, 23 Top, Pavel L Photo and Video, 21, Pressmaster, Cover Bottom, Rob Wilson, 22 Top Left, Studio DMM Photography, Designs & Art, Design Element; SuperStock: Marka, Cover Top, The Francis Frith Collection, 6, 9; Thinkstock: Anton Sokolov, 22 Bottom, Comstock, 18; Wikimedia: NASA, 13.

Every effort has been made to contact copyright holders of material reproduced in this book. Any omissions will be rectified in subsequent printings if notice is given to the publisher.

Some words are shown in bold, **like this**. You can find them in the glossary on page 23.

Contents

What is history in living memory?

Some history happened a very long time ago. Nobody alive now lived through it.

Some history did not happen so long ago.
Our parents, grandparents and adult
friends can tell us how life used to be.
We call this history in living memory.

How has getting around changed in living memory?

Transport has changed a lot since your grandparents were young. There were fewer cars then, so the roads were quieter.

More people walked or rode bikes to get about. Often journeys took longer than they do today.

How did people in the 1950s make long journeys?

In the 1950s, travelling by aeroplane was very expensive. To visit other countries, people often travelled by ship.

Buses and trains were used more for long journeys. Some people went on holiday by **steam train**.

What were cars like in the 1950s?

Cars became more popular in the 1950s. People didn't have to wear a seatbelt or sit in a child seat. Lots of children could squeeze in the back!

When your parents and grandparents were young, there were no **satnav** maps in cars. If they got lost, they had to read a paper map to find their way.

What changes took place in the 1960s?

In 1969, a new aeroplane called Concorde took its first flight. It could fly faster than the speed of sound.

The first astronauts travelled by space rocket in the 1960s. Neil Armstrong was the first person to walk on the Moon.

When did flying become more popular?

In the 1970s, the first jumbo jets began to fly in the skies. They could carry 300 people at a time.

Flying became cheaper and easier for people. Families began travelling to other countries more for holidays.

What were trains like in the 1980s?

More people had cars in the 1980s, but trains were still popular. In the 1980s, high-speed railways were developed. They ran using electricity.

They could take people on long journeys very quickly. Some trains today are even faster.

Does transport cause problems?

In the 1990s, people became worried about so many cars on the roads. Diesel and petrol cause **pollution**. This is harmful to us and to the planet.

Hybrid cars were invented, which could run using electricity as well as petrol. Engineers are still working hard to find ways to power cars that won't harm the environment.

How do you travel today?

So many people travel by car now that traffic jams can be a problem. Some people like to walk or ride bikes, just as people did in the olden days.

Many people still travel by train, but now **steam trains** are just for fun. Aeroplanes can transport people quickly, but some people still like to travel by ship.

Picture quiz

Which of these cars is from the 1950s?

A

B

C

How can you tell?

Picture glossary

pollution
harmful gases in the air

satnav
electronic system in a car that tells you how to get to places

steam train
train that is powered using fire, which heats water to make steam

Find out more

Books

Going on a Trip (Comparing Past and Present),
 Rebecca Rissman (Raintree, 2014)

Talking About the Past (History at Home),
 Nick Hunter (Raintree, 2014)

Website

**www.bbc.co.uk/schoolradio/subjects/history/
britainsince1930s**
Listen to audio clips about transport in the past.

Index